Early Praise for *Braided Spaces*

From the lush title to the first poem's brave missive and the last poem's completion of the song, Jen Cheng explores and re-envisions our understanding of sexual identity, young love, classical music, racialized food, flowers, cultures, and places. This work re-invigorates the poetic lexicon with new, needed music.

Shonda Buchanan, award-winning author of *Black Indian*

In the way that any divination was a search for truth behind existence, Jen Cheng's poems search for a place to call their own against the milieu's dicta predicated upon essentialism, and in doing so, invent a space where myriad cultures (and subcultures) are melded into a state of being that is simultaneously empathetic yet utterly the poet's own. In this empowering collection, the whole globe is ripe for discovery about herself and the world at large—Cheng leans on elemental premonitions as a cornerstone to face difficult personal events and to transcend arbitrary cultural precepts while constructing an identity that is new yet deeply rooted in her ancestry.

Jeremy Ra, 2022 Morton Marcus Poetry Prize,
author of *Another Way of Loving Death*

Jen Cheng utilizes the ancient structure of Feng Shui to craft poems of immense intimacy. This collection of emotional closeness addresses the immigrant experience, growing up female, queerness, and artfully avoids cliché of victimhood or differentness. Cheng's is an original voice of contemplation as she muses and meditates on fishnets, ice cream, mentorship, Hemingway's pipe, and butterflies. As a reader we get to witness her healing and heal in the process. Cheng's Feng Shui focus has created a balanced collection we can inhabit, identify, and take refuge in.

Steven Reigns, First West Hollywood City Poet Laureate,
author of *A Quilt for David*

Step inside the mesmerizing, absorbing, eclectic poems of Jen Cheng's first collection, *Braided Spaces*, and leave with a richer, wider view of yourself and the world. Heartbreaking, funny, intelligent, unexpected—these gems, beautiful and rare, speak in a voice as unique as the experiences written about.

Kim Dower, Second West Hollywood City Poet Laureate
award-winning author of *Sunbathing on Tyrone Power's Grave*

Jen Cheng's *Braided Spaces* is a collection of border crossings, intimate and geographic, threading continents and generations. Informed by Cheng's work as a musician, activist and storyteller, Braided Spaces offers readers more than the act of witness. Cheng's is a world of generous possibilities, where "eager lush magnolia flowers" place personal ads and neighbors might "Feed everyone ... Chinese food as a political act." These are poems with directives, poems that drive us towards coalition, that remind us, if we survive this world, it will be by taking action towards a better one.

Asa Drake, a winner of the 2020 92Y Discovery Poetry Contest,
author of *One Way to Listen*

Jen Cheng's first collection of poems is formally and thematically expansive, organized innovatively around the elements of Feng Shui (wood, fire, water, metal, earth). This gives a flow and narrative bent to these poems of activism, family history, pop culture, and longing. A deep need underlies this collection: the need to be witnessed and understood…This is a book of intersections and discoveries, a diasporic coming-out that flits from New York to Hong Kong to Buenos Aires, a flight where pride and trauma live hand-in-hand. Read this book when you are outraged, when you are lonely, when fast food Chinese and TV reruns just won't cut it. Light a candle. Give yourself permission. See what emerges in this balancing.

Brian Sonia-Wallace, Fourth West Hollywood City Poet Laureate,
author of *The Poetry of Strangers*

Accompany poet Jen Cheng on her journey across time, culture, geography, sexuality, and self-awareness in her chronicle as a world traveler and observer of human nature. At times confessional, at times conspiratorial, this collection throws open windows into Cheng's exploration of her own personhood. She weaves an unsentimental tapestry of her Chinese heritage, her experience of racism and sexism, her evolving queer identity; ultimately, *Braided Spaces* celebrates a woman overcoming, becoming, thriving.

Aruni Wijesinghe, author of *2 Revere Place*

Braided Spaces

jen cheng

Braided Spaces

poems by
jen cheng

wokelicious
press

Braided Spaces

ISBN 979-8-9893846-0-0

Cover design by Jen Cheng
Cover art by Lauren YS
Book Design Support by Wilcox Gwynne and Elena Maria Sanchez
Feng Shui Graphic by Kayte Deioma
Author Photo by Kayte Deioma

Some names have been changed to protect the privacy of individuals.

Wokelicious Press
A Division of Wokelicious LLC
www.wokelicious.com

Printed by
Re/Arte Centro Literario
2123 E. Cesar E. Chavez Ave.
Los Angeles, CA 90033

Distributed in U.S. and internationally by
IngramSpark

First Edition

Dedicated to those who are finding a voice.

Contents

Introduction

Dear Reader,

Over the years, I have struggled to explain my East-West cultural influences as an Asian-American or American-Born Chinese. Everything from the ancient and new-age Buddhist teachings to the post-modern philosophy of queer theory, Critical Race Feminism, and Third World Feminist writing that shaped my early adulthood has led me to my current artivist perspective.

I found a way to play with these East-West influences through a form I developed, "Feng Shui Poetry." I use this form as an event entertainer providing readings from Feng Shui cards and turning people's stories into poetry at art events, weddings, and other community events. In my book, I share my personal poems by organizing them around the Five Elements of Eastern Philosophy: Fire, Earth, Metal, Water, and Wood.

I have a graphic in the Notes at the end for your perusing if you want more information, but I don't want to slow you down at the start. Most people are used to Feng Shui being a method for designing a home or office. While I am not a Feng Shui Master for interior design, I have spent a large part of my adulthood serving as a wellness coach and a spiritual student, so the Five Element lens for understanding our lives (and poetry) is a natural fit for my poetry collection.

A quick overview is that the Five Elements can refer to *how* we approach our lives and, also, they refer to different areas of our life. For example, my friend who has a lot of Fire energy can be very productive in a positive way, enjoys public attention and fame, but can also burn out badly. I have a lot of Earth energy so I'm grounded and provide organizational support when I collaborate with people, but I could benefit from tapping into Fire energy to enjoy more public facing fun. Generally, we benefit from balance.

The way the Five Elements refer to different areas of our lives can be shown in this example:

- Food as fame (fire)
- Food as self-care (earth)
- Food as a precision and beauty (metal)
- Food as career (water)
- Food as feeding family (wood)

My poems each have a dominant element that has influenced where I've placed them in the book. You might interpret a poem differently and perhaps you might assign the poem to a different element. I would be curious hear where you might have assigned a poem differently if you'd like to email me to share.

Braided Spaces is a term I coined by joining two words by my desire to represent a welcome space for intersectionality, for the indivisibility of being who we are with multiple consciousness, and for a coalition-minded community where I don't need to be split into pieces. Like braided hair or braided bread can be seen from different angles where some strands are tucked and less prominent, *braided spaces* celebrates our many dimensions, and in this book, I imagine that we have that depth of appreciation. When I searched the internet for this book title, it turns out "braided spaces" is a term in quantum physics, which I am very fond of.

I promised a book that has themes of immigrant displacement, critical race feminism, and the queer musings of a Chinese American eldest daughter.

A friend pressed me to say something more vulnerable:
This book is written for every girl who has been beaten up for having an opinion.

I don't want us to trauma-bond. Instead, I'm sharing transformation.

This summer, I went to walk with a Writers Guild picket line and my friend found a picket sign that said, "A.I. doesn't have childhood trauma." I took that sign and added on the blank side: "Humans make tragedy into comedy." And also poetry.

I want us to recognize that survivors of domestic violence and bullying might need individualized support to share their points of view. Our points of view. I am deeply thankful to all the kind teachers and supportive people who encouraged me; they provided a lifeline to someone with very low self-esteem. I say piano teachers saved my childhood to give me my first love of music. The English teachers, journalism teachers, and others who encouraged me to write gave me space to find my second love of writing. I have spent my adulthood recovering from childhood, learning through so much throat chakra healing, and continue to do so.

Poetry is a leader in my life that allows me to find community. All survivors need space to be heard. Thank you for wanting to listen.

Your faithful writer and observer,

jen

Fire

Chow Mein in Chiapas

My genetics didn't give me good rhythm
so I learned it from my Afro-Panamanian dance teacher
She'd encourage passionately,
      Eso!   pa- pa- pa - pa - pa!
As I listened to the Cuban beats
I fell in love with Spanish
so I flew to Chiapas to study
like a good hippie

My community college Spanish
gave me good practice on how to order un café
but my Chinese cooking skills earned me
my host family's affection
They asked, "Please cook us authentic chow mein!"
so I went all over town to
to find ingredients and learned
words not in the textbook
like *jingebre*

When I served them chow mein
they politely ate with confusion
and finally asked,
      Porque no cocinas con nopales?
Their local Mexican chow mein came with cactus
so with my elementary Spanish
I said politely, *No pienso que hay nopales in Chine*
And we all had a good laugh

Dance and chow mein
are my passports to bond beyond language
Yut chai sic fan lah!
Bailamos!

7

tell me about dragons
as it happens
i have never tired of dragons
the myths
our fears
our fascinations
restaurants with   dragons in the logo
we know that's where you can reliably get good food
we are all influenced
whether or not you've watched the movie,
The Way of the Dragon
so i'll breathe into the fire
and not worry
that they try to insult me with
labels of *Dragon Lady* meant to
box
me
in.
i take the flight,
the mystery
the powerful red hues
to paint and write
new scrolls and talk story

Painted Painter

I live in a box of paints*
And let them wash over me
Never mind any blurred lines
Different colors tint me each day

Shadows of others from last week
Some of base notes mix and
Mutate into something new
A blend unexpected and leaks

Wisps of quantum light
Dress me in rare treasures like
Lapis Lazuli, gracing eyes
of Cleopatra so intensely

Who wouldn't want admirers
Like royalty, custom made
Tailoring and then catching
Something playful with something sure

So let them call me exotic
I will own it as my mirage
To lure them in like honey wine
Effervescent patterns so rich

Complements and boldness erase
Limits and systems so rigid
Perceptions from every angle
Reflect the multiple faces.

* a line from Joni Mitchell's "A Case of You"

Joseph Schmidt chocolate truffles at the office holiday party

made me question if i was not actually bisexual
and perhaps i was farther over in the lesbian zone
chocolate perky boobs with the perfectly dotted apex
molten centers of flavored crème
melted me with lust
maybe someone will notice my gusto
at the dessert table
look past my too innocent exterior
and ask me out to a dyke extravaganza
most friends saw me as a foodie
but my roommate knew better and laughed
at my sapphic swoon
the mere memory of these now-extinct confections
sets off a wet mouth, tongue ready
for this over affection of cream interiors

Earth

Ceci n'est pas un poème
is an image   of an author
mojitos as my masculine drink so that
at a bar among straight men could get
the mental treachery a female makes
get a crack at a game among lawyers,
with the boys on their turf, learn the
strategies to smoke them defenseless with wits, so
   don't pin a girl to one role of the femme fatale,
      that's a tragedy, that only sexualized power
         could be our raison d'être, to be heroes,
            with eyes closed, appeal to basic
               instinct with a parfum de
                  je ne sais quoi

Hemingway with the pipe
that was a reason to choose
a femme
respect
daily to
wrestle
debate

* inspired by words in wikipedia's entry about Magritte's painting of a pipe,
"The Treachery of Images"

From Rachel*

She thought I was a "poor, raised by a single mother, low-class, immigrant nobody"
and even if I was losing Nick
I was out to show her I am a strong, intelligent somebody.
Not only am I a professor who could command my NYU classroom
But I am also a cultured Chinese American woman in her power
smooth as James Bond, staging a showdown with Mah Jong,
and I proved to Mrs. Crazy Rich, that she was so wrong.
Just because they are the super wealthy did not mean
that I was going to submit to her
especially since
I am the domme of game theory.

*my imagined inner landscape of Rachel Chu from the film, "Crazy Rich Asians"

Loving her from afar

We danced and played among the stars
on sleepy nights, you fly with me
we clash, I sang to give us dreams
you ran, crying no hope for love

You fumble with the keys to my heart
but still, you reach for my wings
you stumble, slipping with the rain
you drowned, I pulled you out of storms

You said you wanted love to last
so, I tuned the sky to play our song
but you guard your heart with your past
you swear what goes up is gonna crash

Even lightning couldn't crack your walls
can you believe together we won't fall
when you're ready, you can catch a ride
can you believe together we won't fall,
we won't fall

I see your armor hiding acid scars
I will always love you
don't you ever think you're just alone
I will always love you

I flew in on a rainbow's light
you didn't trust the clouds would clear
our fight was never black and white
with my wind soar with me

postmodern sapphos*

eager lush magnolia flowers blossom
seek admirers loving the lazy sunday
ready bagels, cream cheese, and mango lassi
newspapers open

hear the cozy morning doves coo and flutter
open windows joining the neighbors' passion
bring on lilts and harmonies sing with pride for
memories later

fluid inspiration that slides from side to
side unfettered gender-free roles that further
child's play with privileged toys to harness
liberty's pleasure

*inspired by the original sapphic form

Metal

Border crossing

A little madness in the spring is wholesome*
even for the responsible daughter
who wanted to wave a subversive middle finger
to the arbitrary racist immigration laws
that had defined her ancestors
and family history.

The spiders of life attempted to weave another immigration story.
This time, her aunt had overstayed her visit
home in Hong Kong and was going to lose her
hard-won U.S. legal immigrant status.
      Mom asked, "Oh dutiful daughter,
      Could you help your aunt cross the Canadian-US border?"
      Born as translator, this daughter said, "Yes, but only if
      Aunt will cooperate and make this successful.
      There's no point in failure."

She recruited a white American software engineer
a guy who was mainstream and worked at Microsoft
to play the part of her boyfriend.
Before 9/11, two US citizens crossing the Canadian border
are easily waved through, especially when
the driver is good-looking,
a professional guy, playing the white chaperone.

All this preparation went to naught, as the anxious aunt
decided it was not worth the trouble to fight.
It was easier to stay an outsider in her native land
than to struggle to learn English and build a new life
on unfriendly American soil.
The aunt might have tried, if she didn't have language barriers,
if maybe she had her own white chaperone.

*first line is from Emily Dickinson.

Mentors with the Letter M

I.

Mina showed me how to play music emotionally
with her passionate but out of tune humming that moaned
as she coaxed the music from her other grand piano
and commanded me to copy what I had just heard

She was the first to teach me how to use my body
how to be physical with another person intimately
as she taught me to wrap my little fingers
to dance on top of her wrinkled hands to imitate how she played

She ruined me for the light keys of easier-to-play Yamahas
and got me to love the thick sounds of the complex Bösendorfers and Steinways
decades later, I feel that heavy hammer action now when I use a typewriter,
light touch keys get jammed with my strong and fast piano fingers

She stopped me from straining my hands too small
to sustain repeated stretched octaves by
introducing me to the Alexander technique
to breathe better and relax between every effort

She affectionately sprinkled Yiddish words into her praise
smother my stiff awkward Chinese body into her passionate Russian Jew hugs
pushing my too short head into her ample bosom,
and transferred more love with rugalach and baklava she put out at recitals

My studies were interrupted too early by my mother's whims
and I couldn't find a way to sneak out to my beloved teacher
it's too late now to find her . . . my best homage to her is
to learn the piece she wanted me to conquer: the piano concerto known as the Rach 3

II.

Marla normalized things I didn't know yet were taboo
I came for freedom of speech, under attack for my underground paper
and found a fondness for leather daddies who met her for drinks at The Stud
and a fascination with her butch girlfriend who picked her up on a motorcycle

She mobilized spirited youth activists as leaders of high school conferences
she taught us facilitation skills, made us fearless public speakers
we took over the Convention Centers like this world belonged to us
and chatted with civil rights lawyers and hippie activists like we were equals

She had us use the copy machines, make banners, staple signs
and gave us stellar office and organizing skills
she played our mixed tapes for the events
as the angsty soundtracks to our peers' memories

She patiently worked on a Saturday so that we could trek in
from everywhere like Redwood City, Walnut Creek to Marin
the BART train was our tunnel to freedom and she let us stay extra late
as she fed us pizza, she knew we needed this space for weirdos, nerds, and geeks

She welcomed me when I arrived as a thirty-something in New York City
not surprised that I was one of many from that cohort who finally came out as queer
she was organizing a Lesbian Feminism conference and put me on
the panel about Sex with her now ex from San Francisco

She saw I was a Third Wave instigator empowered in skirts and three-inch heels and
assigned me to debate with her ex, the Second Wave butch
moderated by a soft tomboy who watched me confuse their old school chivalry
by opening the door first for them to walk in

She continued her role as mentor voluntarily
as she sent me to interview with a Brooklyn radio show
for a post conference debrief, to represent a lesbian perspective
pushing me to be daring, yet again.

Chinese food as a political act

Did you know Chinese food is more American than apple pie?
That more people eat rice than McDonald's French fries?

On a better day, my ability to cook Chinese food
gives me a passport to privilege — privilege to cook
organic and free-range Chinese food for a Bel Air party
for money that helps pay my rent.
Because you can't get organic Chinese food.

Because Americans decided
it's supposed to be cheap fast food,
a decision given the racist history of immigration policy
and importing railroad workers.

On a bad day, I'm told someone doesn't like Chinese food
because "it's greasy,"
and *greasy* feels like not just an insult but another hate word.
Has *greasy* ever been a compliment?

I defend my culture with politeness while seething inside,
patient with cultural ignorance yet again.
A reminder that not everyone bothers to learn about other cultures
and step outside our history of racism and oppression.

So, this nice Chinese girl society expects me to be
asks, "What have you tried?"
And usually they say Panda Express.
"You know, that's fast food, right?"

So I cook homemade fried rice or chow mein
for them to try, and they realize Chinese food isn't just cheap and greasy.
That my culture is something more than egg rolls.

I am expected to take the high road
and not be furious every time I experience
yet another paper cut of ignorance or racism.
Chinese food, my cultural diplomacy
to get people to be curious and
bridge intercultural relations.

It is not enough to live side by side
when we are treated as trash and targets of violence and theft.
I cannot watch one more video of another Asian being beaten or killed.
This mob mentality of taking or trashing.
We are not cheap and not greasy.

Hey Neighbor,
Can we just feed everyone some Chinese food and
have them listen to some anti-racist cultural re-education?
Feed everyone with love so we can stop this nightmare.
Feed them Chinese food as a political act.

At least it wasn't...

On Lunar New Year' day,
I woke up to a text from
my not-so-social East Coast friend
  "Just checking in. I read about the terrible shooting."

My first instinct was to quickly search
"West Hollywood shooting"
while praying very hard,
  "Please don't let it be
  another gay club
  targeted by a hater."

Something about something on Sunset Blvd
turned up on the google search but
at least it wasn't a gay bar targeted last night.

My second step was to look on social media.
What happened?
Instagram gave me the latest about Monterey Park
with no information about the gunman.

I prayed very hard again,
  "Please don't let this be an Anti-Asian hate crime."

I survived through the nineties as a social justice organizer.
I don't want there to be a terrible threat of burning riots.
When I found out it was an Asian gunman,
at least it wasn't a racial attack.

Now can we finally get the spotlight on
toxic masculinity,
mental health,
domestic violence,
and gun control?

"Intersectionality" is not a convenient word
white liberals can throw around
as lip service to say they understand.
The threats,
the survivor traumas,
the thought patterns
        "At least it wasn't…
                            worse"
is how some of us get through
one day at a time.

Water

Ten Thousand Butterflies

How many butterflies had to flutter
to change the weather patterns
enough for my ancestors to survive
to escape the cultural cleansing that was meant
to erase

To erase those who were different
Poh-poh said, *Many did not make it*
especially on your father's side
tailors, those who had skills, too smart, some drowned
They had to swim

Had to swim
across the waters to the British colony
Hong Kong where they made a new life
But why? I asked.
Deem guy ah?

Deem guy?
To survive. To escape the bad guys.
Grandma tried to explain to me when I was only five.
When I was a teen, the Japanese soldiers could have taken me
I had to take the soot

The soot, the burnt black bottom bits of the wok
rubbed it on my face to make me ugly
and claim my older brother as my husband
because the soldiers were likely to take away
the single young pretty girls

Young pretty girls
were taken away during the war
so she had to pretend. It was safer to be ugly.
What if Grandma, Poh-poh, had been taken away
I wouldn't be here today

I wouldn't be here today
if mom didn't marry dad. Because dad
promised Ah-Mah on her deathbed
that he would return to find a bride
back in Hong Kong

Back in Hong Kong
in 1996, I traveled as a college student before the turnover to China
to find my roots, so much missing history,
but my relatives said I had to promise to
Never go to China alone

Never go to China alone, without a tour group to protect you
because you don't speak Mandarin and you stand like an American
anything you say or not say will make you a rebel
For no reason, a lowly policeman can throw you in jail
and you will be disappeared

Disappeared like the *desaparecidos* from the protest songs
of Latin America I sang with my college choir.
Ah, the power of bold gay men in the
streets of Buenos Aires reclaiming the slang "Mariposa."
Cambia, todo cambia.

Cambia, todo cambia.
I found the underground lesbian club in Buenos Aires
down an empty street, down a stairwell to a basement
of an Arcade where I asked a girl to
dance with me

Dance with me?
she and her friends laughed at this Loca, this crazy Chinita
tourist traveling alone, wandering into a club lesbiana
where the police still raided gay clubs
and I could be disappeared, so they drove me home

They drove me home
to Palermo where I was staying with the gay boys
who weren't allowed at the lesbian clubs
but were friends with the proudly out local mariposas who worked
at PlanetOut.com

PlanetOut.com, one of the 1990's gay websites where we hungrily scoured for travel
information to find the fun
and find where we thought we could safely travel
but what about the places that were
not safe?

not safe to be pretty boys or butch girls
I passed as a femme and could claim one of the boys as my husband
for different reasons than Grandma
it's a different kind of war
to survive

To survive the political winds that swing violent,
I now choose to live in a proud gay little haven
where I imagine I walk
without the threat of being disappeared as
I count the miracles of butterflies.

Compliments are not a luxury

I was not allowed to receive compliments as a child.
When someone said I was cute
my mother would respond humbly,
"Nah, the rice bag is prettier than my daughter."

When someone said I was talented
my mother would downplay my piano skills,
even though I was winning awards
"Nah, so and so's daughter is so much better."

When my chemistry teacher gave me an A+
I was proud to tell my father
who didn't respond so I repeated myself louder.
He barely looked up from his newspaper
and said, "So what?"

When I got a full-ride scholarship for a summer academy
my mother said, "Who's going to take care of the kids?"

When I got a job after college with health insurance,
I got myself a therapist, a white Jewish older woman
who took the role of a supportive white parent
who tried to teach me to take a compliment
and practice to simply say, "Thank you."

I told her it felt false. I had trouble believing
compliments were real.
She said, "If you can't do it for yourself, do it for their sake.
You're rejecting someone, someone trying to give you a compliment."

I give compliments to other people easily because I appreciate them.
So, OK. I will practice saying thank you
until one day it might feel real.

I'm happy to give a compliment to the grocery bagger
when he does a good game of Tetris with my vegetables
or to the tomboi with the mohawk about her fresh shave.

It's been decades since that first therapist
and I still have some trouble believing
and receiving compliments.

It wasn't until recently that I heard a Chinese elder
say to me, "I'm proud of you."
Speaking through an Aussie psychic
my paternal grandfather
deceased before I was born
sent me love, I felt with my tears.

Compliments are not a luxury.

Waverly

San Francisco Chinatown grocery shopping every weekend
and I would see the street
Waverly Place
while being my mother's sherpa
carrying the too heavy 25 lb bag of rice
or the many bags of bok choy and char siu
on my runt child body of less than 50 lbs.

When I saw the movie Joy Luck Club
with the daughters who suppressed or
expressed their rebellion
I think of how my life was not that movie
I didn't get my reconciliation
or hug – did Chinese mothers hug?

When my Pinay drag king friend
met me on a party boat in New York City
and decided we should be friends,
she nicknamed me "Waverly."
Yes, I was fresh off the boat
from San Francisco
and will always bond
with the daughters of
Joy Luck Club.
Every time I see the movie,
with bone deep tears I want to feel
that proud hug from a Chinese mother as if
I was Waverly.

Spirit Injury*

the law killed my muses
they haunt me
with micro-discrimination
that is
spirit murder

dumbfounded
by offhand manners
not allowed to discuss it
thousands of spirit injuries
dismiss me

no longer merely the sum of separate parts
the multiplier effect
is our multilayered experience

shifting back and forth
between consciousness
tired of being a second-class citizen
waiting to be upgraded to first class
to celebrate
to flourish with richness
here, seen in full reflections,
my muse returns
red for love

*found poem from "Brief Reflections toward
Multiplicative Theory and Praxis of Being," by Adrien Katherine Wing

Fight for the life of a girl*

the terrorist practice of
valuing women as only
bearers of sons

deliberate killing of girl babies
persistent devaluation of female life
criminalized but still the norm

what if more women
exercised their power to disbelieve
that home is not a shrine of violence

uproot culture
speak not on behalf but powerfully
their own words and music

to love their daughters
welcomed with tears of
joy

*found poem from "Female Infanticide in China," by Sharon K. Hom

Job requirement: fishnets or pantyhose

In that split second
the splinter under the desk that snagged my pantyhose
decided the course of my young adult life
It was only 10am and the second of five interviews
to win a job offer with golden handcuffs so
I could cash in on my economics degree
But the rip without the immediate defense of clear nail polish
was only going to grow into an embarrassing tear
that kept running for the rest of the day

The well-meaning classmates who primed me for this rat race
told me the gray-haired partners at the big bank
had conservative standards, that women could not wear pantsuits
because pantsuits were too liberal
Those guys could never understand this extra burden of wardrobe anxiety

As a dancer, it was easier for me to wear fishnets
Danskin made them extra durable, heavyweight
and if they snagged, the rip just added to the sexy look
As a halfway decent second violinist who could dance and wear a wig,
I was recruited to play for a corporate band with travel perks to
a castle in Quebec City and a beachfront hotel in Kawaii

I broke down crying to my philosophy professor
over my feminist angst of these choices, band or bank
the difference of one consonant
what are my roles after being a college student
but to be objectified as a sexy siren
or to fit in a box as a dutiful capitalist

The queer professor shook her head with no advice while
standing in her comfortable shoes
Rousseau nor anything else in my books would help me

The splinter made the decision
since I couldn't wipe the worry about the pantyhose off my face
or remember enough from the sports page
to bond with the bank bro's

KC and the Sunshine Band's medley gave me long whole notes to shake my booty
to play for the bankers at night
or tech bros celebrating the Star Wars prequel
I found a day job crunching
Census data at a think tank, the closest thing to staying in college
at an office with a loose dress code, free from pantyhose
at dark, I changed into a wig, tiny short shorts, and fishnets that didn't tear
for a road more travelled.

Wood

From the first time I tried to be pregnant

You left your haphazard remodel
widened my hips to tell me you were here
I put on pants that can't pull up and instantly remember
I never got to hold you

You were the seed of a story that could have been
and maybe you might find me again
until then I keep trying to run from tears
I never got to hold you

You stayed just long enough to let me know
I deserved to be a mother
hormonal wobbly walks made me smile even though
I never got to hold you

You didn't stay long enough to let me see you
I was with the wrong partner, you told me so
then left to save me from a life of terror
I never got to hold you

You would be nine today like my student
I finish laughing with her jokes and wonder
what songs we might have sung even if
I never got to hold you

You sometimes visit me in dreams
I long for notches on the wall that measure your height
I still wear wide maternity dresses too big and empty when
I never got to hold you

Bridgerton's Narrator Spills the T(ea) about My Grandma*

Grandma dearly departed with a Grand
Hurrah, hailing respect instead of grief
In turn, her memorial party was her dream birthday celebration, as she
Just died gracefully of heart failure in her sleep
Kind of a quiet exit but so obvious as her
Last symphony.
Manipulation was her modus operandi, so
None of her surviving seven children could say No to showing up
Over all the years of plots she orchestrated to stoke
Personality struggles with believable lies as the Drama
Queen and Mother Mastermind of
Recurring rivalries between
Siblings. You needed the latest headlines to know who was mad at whom in this
Telenovela that could outdrink other families
Under the table. Air
Violins would play to
Whine about one sister's injustice or how
Xenophobia ruined a brother's attempts at a white-collar career.
Yarn skeins were what she left behind with a
Zoetic puzzle of where she might have hidden her jewelry.
Accumulated hiding places were ways to anchor her
Bravery through war occupation and poverty as she silently sang her survival song.
Conducting her power even from beyond, her heirs cleaned her home,
Dug through every jacket, looking for secret pockets,
Ever reminded how this frail elder knew how to perform her
Finale.

*imagine reading this with Lady Whistledown's British accent if you may

Mother Tree in Franklin Canyon

three long majestic trunks spread like loving arms
from a base so strong, endlessly holding up the sky
you welcome me every time i visit
and lay my troubles on the bed of your skin
it's so easy to soak up the light through your lacy canopy
to live in an altered space for a little while
your reliable presence helps me find the divine mother
never absent, never overbearing
you are my pillar
giving spacious sure strength
while others have fallen from their duties
you step in ready to love and cherish all
highways of busy ants
stashes of squirrel nuts
pairs of camouflaged birds
you are the shelter for any lost child

Ice Cream Scar

they wanted to take me out for drinks on
my birthday but really
ice cream would be better
i bet you don't know anyone else who has an ice cream scar
right here, see, this eyebrow? it won't grow hair here
because of a happy dance i did when i was too young to remember
my mother says she brought home an ice cream cone
i ran around wildly and tripped into a piece of furniture
and banged my head, lucky i didn't lose my eye

(and i pray that this is a true story because
i want to feel the pure joy
of that little girl too innocent before she knew the
pain of choked and silenced laughter
i need this story to be true to find that runaway soul
this is the one proud scar i share)

they said, let's have you sit down for your ice cream
we worry about others drunk driving on their birthday
we can't lose a poet with a trip and fall

For the immigrant social worker who left her barrio

We dance and grow as daffodils
in streets not meant for us, estranged
where knives and guns pierced every day
survival stemmed from strength and will.
Our budding smiles beamed out hope
as woven webs of haunting dreams
to leave again a refugee
and build new life but wanting home.

Still I stand

Still I stand
not like a tree
the way my mother told me
but like a dandelion
more scrappy, wild, and free
surprising people
in the harsh cold of impossibilities
I incubate in disguise
underestimated as a little thing
and spread the blanket of my tribe
We bloom in unfriendly places
season after season
Still I speak undeniably
with dandelion fields of gold.

Notes

There are many schools of Feng Shui practitioners. I have made this graphic based on what I have researched as a general map of how I understand the Five Elements.

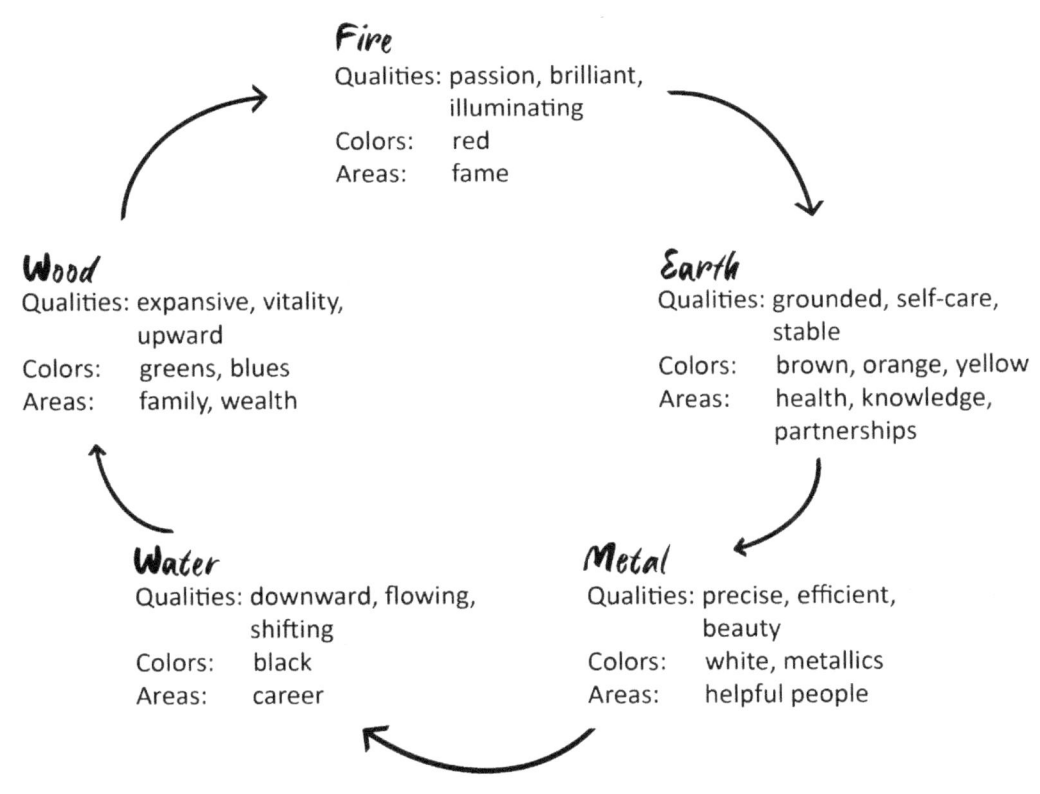

Fire
Qualities: passion, brilliant, illuminating
Colors: red
Areas: fame

Earth
Qualities: grounded, self-care, stable
Colors: brown, orange, yellow
Areas: health, knowledge, partnerships

Wood
Qualities: expansive, vitality, upward
Colors: greens, blues
Areas: family, wealth

Metal
Qualities: precise, efficient, beauty
Colors: white, metallics
Areas: helpful people

Water
Qualities: downward, flowing, shifting
Colors: black
Areas: career

<u>Other Notes</u>
(in the order of the poems)

Painted Painter quotes "I live in a box of paints" from:
"Case of You," by Joni Mitchell, https://jonimitchell.com/music/song.cfm?id=181

Ceci n'est pas un poème uses words from the Wikipedia entry of Magritte's painting, *The Treachery of Images*:
https://en.wikipedia.org/wiki/The_Treachery_of_Images

From Rachel refers to the character Rachel Chu from the film, *Crazy Rich Asians*:
https://en.wikipedia.org/wiki/Crazy_Rich_Asians_(film)

postmodern sapphos is inspired by the original sapphic form:
https://poets.org/glossary/sapphic

Border crossing quotes a line from "A little madness in the Spring" by Emily Dickinson:
https://www.emilydickinsonmuseum.org/a-little-madness-in-the-spring-1356/

Spirit injury is a found poem from:
Wing, Adrien Katherine. *Brief Reflections toward Multiplicative Theory and Praxis of Being* in Critical Race Feminism (Adrien Katherine Wing, 1997)

Fight for the life of a girl is a found poem from:
Hom, Sharon K. *Female Infanticide in China* in Critical Race Feminism (Adrien Katherine Wing, 1997)

My intention when I wrote these found poems from *Critical Race Feminism* is to reach a larger audience of people who might not read legal theory so that wisdom from legal scholars can be more accessible.

Acknowledgements

Thank you to those who encouraged me to put together this book project when I found out that I was selected as the Fifth West Hollywood Poet Laureate in April 2023. It has been a race to grow, write, and publish this book in these few short months for an October release. I couldn't have produced this collection without the swift response of my supporters. I especially want to give my deep, heartfelt appreciation to my very accomplished reviewers who stepped forward to give me early praise, finding time for me in their busy poet lives and travel schedules: West Hollywood Poets Laureate Steven Reigns, Kim Dowers, Brian Sonia-Wallace; and new poet friends Shonda Buchanan, Jeremy Ra, Asa Drake, and Aruni Wijesinghe.

The foundation of this book is thanks to the early encouragement of those who helped shape my first ten poems for fellowships and application packets before my selection as Poet Laureate: editors Emily Schultz and Faye Guenther. Thank you, Faye, for asking great questions and your continued support to see this collection from beginning to end. Other friends who provided editing and revision support were invaluable to the wordsmithing necessary to clarifying my messages: Gil Groom, Ash Nichols, Kayte Deioma, and Bonnilee Kaufman.

So much admiration and appreciation to the artist who gave me permission to use their beautiful visual creation: Lauren YS painted the mural art that graces my cover. Thank you to designers Wilcox Gwynne and Elena Maria Sanchez for helping me bring to life the visuals I imagined. Kayte Deioma has pitched in every way, from being a great photographer to saving my sanity with design advice and details.

Thank you to my lawyer and friend Ghen Laraya Long for steadfast support and strategic thinking on this project and my other writing projects. To my chosen sister, Chiray Koo: So much gratitude to you for being a pillar of strength with logistical and spiritual support, especially when I have been most challenged.

My unending gratitude to those who create cultural spaces that allowed me to grow as an artist. Mike Che and WeHo Arts has nurtured a local culture where LGBTQ creatives feel welcomed. Brian Sonia-Wallace is fearless leader of the Pride Poets project where I immediate fell in love with typewriter poetry, an art of writing custom poems, which has helped me find greater flow and a community of friends. My last four years of writing depended on cultural leaders like Mike and Brian who produced innovative events that nurture the creative spirit. As I witnessed these cultural leaders create new spaces, I was able to bring Palabras Literary Salon to life with the help of Andi Xoch of Latinx with Plants as my co-host, and I am so grateful for all the poets and writers who have come together in my vision of intercultural community. This kind of space is what gives me hope that all our multiple identities can be celebrated together, woven together, to make what I call, *braided spaces.*

So much gratitude for the recommendation letters and words of encouragement from all the thoughtful and caring teachers and mentors who got me here; you know who you are if you're reading this, thank you from the depths of my heart. You are what I call everyday heroes. I especially want to thank my first writing mentor Jim Mattson, who has an open-door policy to answer my questions. When I asked him to fill the role when we first met at an LGBTQ pool party over twelve years ago, he generously said yes to an eager stranger. I explained that I really wanted to be a writer, but I didn't know exactly how, but I knew I needed someone I could talk to.

The road has been bumpy, and I am deeply grateful to those who forged ahead of me to give me hope. Thank you doesn't say enough to those who have kept me alive with words of support, meals, and dog care, especially when I was in medical crisis. Writing and poetry has been part of my healing.

Many thanks for the scholarships and grants that have helped me along the way. Most recently, I have been fortunate to win a few scholarship lotteries to attend online craft intensives with Tin House Workshop that have improved my technical skills and gave me the opportunity to meet colleagues Asa Drake and Ash Nichols. Great gratitude for the California Arts Council Fellowship money, which arrived just in time to help me pay for the production of this book. The financial support from private gifts and public grants is essential to an emerging artist like me.

Thank you to all of you who have been my butterflies, helping me with efforts small and big: your kindness has brought me miracles to help me bring this book to life.

JEN CHENG is the Fifth West Hollywood Poet Laureate, a 2023 California Arts Council Fellow, and a multidisciplinary storyteller who amplifies under-represented voices. Jen is the founder of Palabras Literary Salon, celebrating BIPOC poets and writers. Jen blends East-West cultural influences in a new form, Feng Shui Poetry. With stories for tween audiences, mystery detective fans, and queer love, Jen is a cross-pollinator. Find her on Twitter/IG @JenCvoice or: www.JenCvoice.com

www.ingramcontent.com/pod-product-compliance
Lightning Source LLC
Chambersburg PA
CBHW082112120626
46553CB00011B/3649